ESSENTIAL
BATHROOMS

TERENCE
CONRAN
ESSENTIAL
BATHROOMS

THE BACK TO BASICS GUIDE TO HOME DESIGN, DECORATION & FURNISHING

conran OCTOPUS

Contents

14

Planning & Layout

INTRODUCTION

Introduction

In recent years, as our homes have become ever more important as refuges from the stresses and strains of everyday life, the bathroom has emerged as the refuge within the refuge. Although the primary purpose of the bathroom remains the same – first and foremost to serve as a place to get clean – its role as a private sanctuary now comes a very close second.

Not so long ago, this was very far from the case. While North American bathrooms have always been more generous and more efficient than those in Europe, most bathrooms a few decades ago were still relatively small. In areas where a large proportion of the housing stock dates back a century or more, bathrooms were often introduced into existing layouts in a somewhat ad hoc fashion and generally occupied quite cramped locations. Even in new homes, it was not unusual for the bathroom to be 'the smallest room'. In many cases, a certain coyness about bodily functions made them clinical, if not faintly forbidding places, designed and fitted for utility rather than comfort. They were certainly not rooms where anyone might be encouraged to linger.

All this has changed. Bathrooms have not only grown bigger and more numerous, they have also become the focus of considerable design attention. What the trade calls 'sanitary ware' used to be almost exclusively made of glazed ceramic, which limited sizes and shapes. Now there is an incredible breath of choice, with bathtubs and sinks reinvented as expressive sculptural elements in materials such as wood, glass and stone. Fittings in new shapes and sizes – cornered, angled, tapered, over-scale – are also

available thanks to the use of acrylic, which means that it is easier than ever before to cope with awkward or difficult layouts.

Above all, bathrooms have now become places where we expect to enjoy spending time. The use of evocative surfaces and finishes, from mosaic and limestone to glass and hardwood, spells out the same message of quality one would expect elsewhere in the home, along with a tactile dimension appropriate in a space where we spend a good deal of time unclothed. Increasingly, features that one would normally expect only to encounter in a health club or spa are beginning to appear on the domestic scene, as well: power showers with massaging water

ABOVE: BLACK-AND-WHITE CHEQUERED TILING MAKES A GRAPHIC BACKDROP IN A TOP-LIT BATHROOM.

LEFT: A SCULPTURAL STONE BATHTUB, WITH A FREESTANDING FILLER TAP AND SHOWER, BRINGS AN ELEMENTAL QUALITY TO THE EXPERIENCE OF BATHING.

continued

Introduction

jets, whirlpool baths, steam and sauna rooms. These may be expensive but nowadays are by no means uncommon.

One of the greatest changes, perhaps, is the greater visibility of the bathroom. The fully waterproofed wet room that expresses the elemental experience of bathing, along with open-plan bedroom/bathrooms where the separation between functions is minimal, bring a refreshing new dimension to design approaches.

Whatever your requirements, budget or personal preferences, good planning is essential. In other areas of the home, it is perfectly possible to adopt a more piecemeal approach and acquire furniture and furnishings over a period of time. As an essentially fitted area, however, with fixed elements connected to a servicing infrastructure, the bathroom should be conceived as a whole in order to make the most efficient use of the space you have available. Certain other practical aspects, from lighting to heating, also demand different solutions than those you would employ elsewhere. Then, too, there is the need to address water consumption, a factor that is becoming ever more critical in these environmentally conscious times.

The bathroom plays a key role in our daily routines. Whatever its size or shape and whichever fittings you choose, a successful design is one that fosters a sense of well-being.

ABOVE: WET ROOMS, WHERE SHOWERS DRAIN DIRECTLY INTO THE FLOOR, HAVE BECOME AN INCREASINGLY POPULAR DESIGN OPTION.

RIGHT: IN THIS FAMILY BATHROOM, OCCUPYING PART OF A CONVERTED ATTIC, THE BATHTUB AND TOILET ARE NEATLY INTEGRATED WITHIN A BUILT-IN FRAMEWORK.

Assessing your needs

Whether you are creating a new bathroom or upgrading an existing one, thorough planning is vital. Bathrooms are essentially fitted areas and mistakes can be expensive to remedy. Begin by thinking about your personal requirements as well as your preferences.

■ How many bathrooms do you need? Installing an additional bathroom or cloakroom can radically improve a family's daily routine.
■ If the bathroom is to be shared, who will be using it? Children and the elderly or less able have specific needs. You may wish to consider installing double sinks to ease the strain in family bathrooms or wall-hung fittings to make a cloakroom more accessible for a wheelchair.

■ Which features do you want to include aside from bath/shower, toilet and sink?
■ How much storage do you think you will require? Most bathroom storage is fitted, which means that it needs to be considered at the beginning.
■ Do you need to keep laundry appliances in your bathroom?
■ What type of mood are you trying to create? Are you attracted by the elemental quality of a wet room or do you want a bathroom where you can linger for a long soak?
■ How important is privacy? Bathrooms and showers can be sited within bedrooms or minimally partitioned from them if you are comfortable baring all.

ABOVE: WALL-MOUNTED TAPS AND HAND-HELD SHOWERS ARE VISUALLY NEAT. HARDWOOD CLADDING COMPLETES THIS STREAMLINED DESIGN.

RIGHT: STORAGE IS A KEY CONSIDERATION IN THE BATHROOM. THESE ADJUSTABLE SHELVES PROVIDE AN ATTRACTIVE PLACE TO KEEP TOWELS.

Siting & structure

Existing conditions will dictate how far your requirements can be met. These include the amount of space at your disposal and how the plumbing is arranged.

- If space is limited, consider borrowing extra room from adjoining areas, such as a hallway. Even a small amount of additional space can make the difference between a layout that is workable and one that is not.
- If your plans entail increasing the weight on an existing floor by installing a heavier bathtub or a heavy flooring material, you may need to check that the floor is strong enough.
- If you are planning to include wall-hung fixtures, you need to check that the wall structure is strong enough to support them.
- Check local planning and building regulations to ensure that your plans comply. In many areas, it is illegal for toilets to be directly accessible from an area where food is eaten or prepared.
- Bathrooms do not require windows, but adequate ventilation or mechanical extraction is still necessary.
- It is important to make sure that a new bathroom is easily accessible.
- If your plans necessitate structural change, you will need the services of a surveyor or design professional.
- Changes to drainage will need to be inspected and approved. New servicing connections need to be made by the relevant utility.

ABOVE: IF YOU HAVE ENOUGH SPACE IN YOUR HOME, IT CAN BE WORTH CONVERTING A SMALL BEDROOM TO MAKE A GENEROUS BATHROOM.

LEFT: SLOTTED TEAK MAKES PRACTICAL AND SLIP-RESISTANT FLOORING IN A WET AREA, ALLOWING WATER TO DRAIN AWAY UNDERNEATH.

Basic plumbing

Water supply

The two main types of plumbing system are direct and indirect. In the direct system, which is common in North America and Europe, cold potable water under mains pressure is supplied directly to sinks, bathtubs, showers and toilets. All cold taps supply drinking water and there is always enough pressure for showering, wherever the shower is located. In the indirect system, common in Britain, particularly in older properties, water is supplied via a rising main that feeds the cold-water kitchen tap and a storage cistern. The cold-water kitchen tap is the only supply of drinking water. The cistern must be 3m (10ft) above the showerhead to supply sufficient water pressure. Whatever the system, water pipes should be easy to conceal and branch as little as possible.

Drainage

Waste water and sewage drains either to the main sewer (in urban areas) or to a septic tank. Waste pipes need to slope at a required angle, which means that bathroom fixtures cannot be sited too far away from the main drainage stack. Toilets must be connected directly to the soil pipe, which must be ventilated and extended beyond windows and roof level.

ABOVE: A SMALL PORCELAIN BASIN WITH WALL-MOUNTED TAPS SITS ON TOP OF A RUSTIC-STYLE COUNTER MADE OF WANEY-EDGED WOOD.

RIGHT: ROSE SHOWERHEADS ENSURE PLENTY OF WATER IS DELIVERED. WHERE WATER PRESSURE IS LOW, A SHOWER MAY NEED TO BE PUMP-ASSISTED.

Budgeting & buying

When buying a bathroom, set a notional budget in place at the outset. Draw up a shopping list of preferences, cost them and think about where savings can be made. Do not compromise on the basic quality of fixtures and fittings. It may be better to do without a bidet, for example, if it means you can afford a better quality bathtub, toilet and sink. The choice of materials for surfaces and finishes offers the greatest scope for financial juggling. Watch out for hidden costs, such as professional fees, and unforeseen events, such as if plumbers discover that the existing pipework is not as they imagined.

- Many large stores that supply bathroom fittings and fixtures also provide a range of other services, including in-house design, installation and financial packages.
- Bathroom specialists are more likely to stock designer ranges or fittings and fixtures in unusual materials such as wood, stone and glass. Many such retailers will also design your bathroom for you and will take responsibility for keeping costs within your budget.
- If you are after a period look, salvage yards often stock reclaimed sinks and bathtubs.
- If the work is complex or entails structural change, you might consider employing an architect or designer to come up with a scheme for you and coordinate the services of plumbers, electricians and builders.

ABOVE: FITTINGS IN UNUSUAL MATERIALS SUCH AS STONE AND WOOD ARE GENERALLY MORE EXPENSIVE THAN STANDARD MODELS.

LEFT: THE LARGE SLATE TILES CLADDING THIS SHOWER MAKE AN EFFECTIVE CONTRAST TO THE BUSIER GRID OF SMALL WHITE CERAMIC TILES USED ELSEWHERE.

Designing the layout

Whether you are seeking professional advice or going it alone, it is a good idea to draw up an initial floor plan.

- Make a rough sketch, marking on the position of existing features, such as windows, light fixtures and doors.
- Take accurate measurements of the available space and label the sketch.
- Create a scale plan on graph paper using the information from your sketch plan. A scale of 1:20 is appropriate for bathrooms.
- Using the same scale, you can cut out templates of various bathroom fixtures and move them around to experiment with different layouts.
- If the ceiling slopes, you may also need to make a scale drawing of each wall.
- Bathroom fittings come in a range of shapes and sizes. A key consideration is providing enough space around each fixture for easy access and comfortable use.
- Provide some separation between the toilet and the bathtub. At least ensure that the toilet does not align with the head of the tub.
- The position of the toilet can be a good starting place when planning a layout. If the area is already plumbed, there may be few choices where the toilet can be sited.
- Another starting point might be the position of the bathtub, since this represents the largest element.
- Both toilets and bathtubs can be sited under sloping ceilings, provided there is adequate clearance at the front.

ABOVE: WHEN SPACE IS TIGHT, YOU NEED TO ENSURE THAT THE LAYOUT ALLOWS ENOUGH SPACE AROUND EACH FITTING FOR EASY ACCESS.

RIGHT: A GENEROUS DOUBLE SINK IN THE FORM OF A STONE TROUGH FITS NEATLY INTO A RECESS WITH ROOM FOR STORAGE UNDERNEATH.

Design approaches

Nowadays the bathroom is a room in its own right, not merely a functional place for ablutions. This shift in emphasis means that there is now a much wider choice of bathroom fittings and fixtures and a broader approach to bathroom design as a whole.

To some extent, the size of the space at your disposal will dictate the design approach that is most suitable to take. Smaller bathrooms are best fully fitted, both to integrate the separate elements in a harmonious whole and to make the most of available space. If you have more room to play with, the layout can be more dynamic and feature freestanding furniture and fittings. Most inclusive is the bathroom sited within a bedroom, with minimal separation between the two – the 'en suite' arrangement taken to its furthest extent.

The bathroom is defined by its prime function, which means basic practicality is the bottom line. At the same time, personal preference should also come into play. The bathroom should be a place where you enjoy spending time. Sensitive lighting, good quality surfaces and finishes and attention to detail are just as important here as they are in the rest of the home.

LEFT: BLUE MOSAIC TILES REMINISCENT OF A SWIMMING POOL MAKE AN EVOCATIVE BACKDROP IN A WET ROOM FITTED WITH AN OVER-SCALED SHOWERHEAD.

ABOVE: A TRADITIONAL FREESTANDING CLAW-FOOT BATHTUB MAKES A SUITABLE FOCAL POINT IN A BATHROOM WITH A FURNISHED APPEARANCE.

Large bathrooms

Whether a bathroom is large in its own right or forms part of a bigger inclusive space, generosity of scale goes a long way to promoting a feeling of relaxation. When you have plenty of room to play with, the options for layout are dramatically increased and fixtures need not be wall-hugging.

Layout

- Think about siting the bathtub in a prominent position, either centrally, projecting at right angles from the wall or in front of a window.
- Different levels can be very dynamic. A bathtub can be raised up a level or sunk into the floor. Building a platform in order to sink a bathtub within it is the best way of achieving this.

- Sinks are best sited along a wall to make plumbing runs neater.
- In open-plan bedroom/bathrooms, the bathroom can be sited behind a half-height or half-width partition that doubles up as an over-scaled headboard.
- If your bathroom is large, you might think about using it as a dressing area as well, building a wall of seamless cupboards customized with shelving, hanging rails and cubbyholes to house your wardrobe.
- Good ventilation is essential, backed up by mechanical extraction if necessary, particularly if you are showering or bathing in the room where you also sleep.

ABOVE: A CONTEMPORARY BATHTUB IS PROMINENTLY SITED IN FRONT OF A LARGE WINDOW IN A BATHROOM IMMEDIATELY ADJOINING A MASTER BEDROOM.

RIGHT: A MODERN INTERVENTION IN A TRADITIONAL ROOM, A SHOWER IS MINIMALLY SCREENED FROM A FREESTANDING BATHTUB BY A SHEET OF PLATE GLASS.

continued

Large bathrooms

Fixtures & furnishing

Large bathrooms demand fittings and fixtures that are worthy of scrutiny. In particular, the focus falls on the bathtub. Sculptural designs, from roll-top, claw-foot period pieces to contemporary oval or round bathtubs, look good enough to take centre stage. Vessel-like bowls or troughs are also more appealing than standard sinks in rooms where they are out on view.

Greater floor area means that large bathrooms can be furnished with additional pieces of freestanding furniture. Armoires and chests can double up as storage for linen; the odd chair, chaise longue or bench emphasises the relaxed atmosphere. In the same vein, you should also pay attention to lighting: dimmable lights allow you to vary the mood for a long soak.

Surfaces & finishes

In a small bathroom where fittings are close together, surfaces and finishes must be waterproof and easy to keep clean. Where the layout is more generous, you can choose from a broader selection.

A key surface is the floor. Where the bathroom is en suite, or forms part of an inclusive bedroom/bathroom, it is important to think about the space as a whole. Either choose a flooring material that can be extended throughout or combine materials that are tonally very similar, such as natural-fibre or wood flooring for the sleeping part of the room and tile, stone or mosaic in the wet areas.

ABOVE: PERIOD DESIGNS, SUCH AS THIS CLAW-FOOT BATHTUB, LOOK GOOD IN TRADITIONAL SETTINGS. HERE, THE FLOORBOARDS HAVE BEEN SEALED WITH WATER-RESISTANT PAINT.

LEFT: A PAIR OF DOUBLE SINKS SIT ATOP AN EXTENSIVE WASHSTAND THAT PROVIDES STORAGE BELOW FOR TOWELS AND PERSONAL ACCESSORIES.

Family bathrooms

Family bathrooms are, by definition, shared spaces. Unsurprisingly, they work best when space is generous and there is room to build in enough storage to take care of everyone's needs. At certain critical times of the day, such as early morning or during the wind-down to bedtime, bottlenecks may occur. A larger room allows you to double up sinks or provide a separate shower as well as a bath, which can help to ease congestion. Family bathrooms are also good places for laundry machines, making shorter work of a routine chore.

Layout, fixtures & fittings

- Keep it simple and focus on safety when planning the bathroom layout and choosing fixtures and fittings.
- It is often a good idea to base the layout around the position of the bathtub. You will need extra clearance around or alongside the bathtub for kneeling or bending over to supervise small children during bath time.
- Choose acrylic or ceramic fixtures and fittings, rather than those in materials such as steel, glass or stone, which are harder to maintain. Rounded edges are safer than sharp corners.
- Thermostatic controls reduce the risk of accidental scalding.
- Provide booster steps to allow small children to access sinks easily.

ABOVE: TRANSLUCENT PANELS CONCEAL GENEROUS BUILT-IN STORAGE BELOW DOUBLE SINKS. MOSAIC CLADDING UNIFIES THE ENTIRE SPACE.

RIGHT: A LARGE DOUBLE-ENDED WOODEN BATHTUB IS THE FOCAL POINT OF THIS FAMILY BATHROOM.

continued

Family bathrooms

Surfaces & finishes

Most small children approach bathing as a form of water play, which means that surfaces and finishes should be fully waterproof, easy to keep clean and as non-slip as possible. Even when children are older, a shared bathroom is going to see more frequent use and require a higher degree of maintenance. Surfaces and finishes should be as smooth and seamless as possible to provide less opportunity for grime to build up. Wood panelling, ceramic tiles and mosaic make practical wall cladding; linoleum, vinyl, cork and rubber work well on the floor. If you want to tile the floor, choose a ceramic tile with a matt finish or use mosaic, which is less slippery.

Storage

- Pegs and racks are a good way of organizing personal care items. Colour-coded containers make it easy to distinguish whose is whose.
- You will need secure, lockable storage for bleach and bathroom cleansers. Medicine cabinets should be positioned out of children's reach and also kept locked.
- Separate drawers or modular containers provide an unobtrusive way of housing shampoos, lotions and other bathroom products. Not every one in the family is going to share the same preferences and a skyline of different bottles around the bathtub looks untidy and makes cleaning awkward.

LEFT: DOUBLE SINKS HELP TO EASE CONGESTION IN FAMILY BATHROOMS AT BUSY TIMES OF THE DAY.

FAR LEFT: IN A CONVERTED ATTIC, A BATH IS SITED UNDER THE SLOPING CEILING, KEEPING THE FLOOR AREA CLEAR WHERE THERE IS GREATER HEAD HEIGHT.

Small bathrooms

Designing a small bathroom is undoubtedly a challenge, but with careful planning you need not compromise on function or looks. What you may have to sacrifice, however, is any fitting or fixture that is not strictly necessary. When space is limited, you may wish to forego a bidet, and laundry appliances will almost certainly need to go elsewhere. While showers are more space-saving than bathtubs, the extra floor area will not be much of a bonus if taking a long hot bath is your favourite way to relax.

Layout, fixtures & fittings

- First investigate whether it is possible to increase the floor area, even if only by a small amount. You might be able to move a partition wall forwards a short distance, which could make the difference between a cramped layout and one that is workable.
- If your bathroom has a pair of windows, blocking up one of them might win you additional wall space for a shower or heated towel rail.
- Sliding panels or screens are more space-saving than doors. Alternatively, a door can be rehung to open outwards.
- Many manufacturers produce ranges of fixtures that are either more compact than standard or shaped to make the best use of the available space.
- Wall-hung sinks and toilets keep the floor area clear, creating a more spacious feel.

ABOVE: A MIRROR IS A USEFUL WAY OF ENHANCING THE SENSE OF SPACE.

RIGHT: WALL-HUNG AND BACK-TO-THE-WALL FITTINGS ARE VISUALLY NEAT, AS ARE WALL-MOUNTED TAPS.

continued

Small bathrooms

Decorative strategies

- In a small bathroom, you should keep decorative schemes simple and coordinated.
- Extend tiling and other types of cladding to cover whole walls, rather than introduce uncomfortable visual breaks.
- Junctions and edges where one type of material meets another should be as neat and inconspicuous as possible. Single seamless flooring or large tiles can be more space-enhancing than a busy grid of smaller tiles.
- Reflective surfaces, such as glass and metal, help to spread around available light.
- A sheet of mirror placed opposite a window, or a pair of mirrors on facing walls, enhances space and makes the most of light.
- Spotlights or small recessed downlights placed around the perimeter of the room will increase the sense of breadth.

Storage

- Integrating fixtures within a built-in framework provides coherence and allows you to exploit spaces between fixtures for storage.
- Clutter is distracting and undermines the sense of space. Restrict what you leave on view to the bare minimum.
- Glass shelves are less dominating than ones made of opaque materials.
- In a really small bathroom, you may have to store linen and bathroom products elsewhere.
- Heated towel rails double up as towel storage and a heat source. In a small bathroom, you might not need any additional heating.

ABOVE: TREATING ALL SURFACES AND FINISHES UNIFORMLY IS A GOOD STRATEGY FOR SMALL BATHROOMS. WHITE ENHANCES A SENSE OF SPACE.

LEFT: IF SPACE IS REALLY TIGHT, YOU MIGHT CONSIDER DOING WITHOUT A BATHTUB AND OPTING FOR A GENEROUS WALK-IN SHOWER INSTEAD.

Awkward shapes

Sloping ceilings

Lack of head height, in a converted attic space, for example, can pose limitations on layout. Provided there is enough space to access the bathtub without cracking your head on a beam, it can be sited where the ceiling slopes down, making use of what would otherwise be redundant space under the eaves. Similarly, a toilet does not require full head height, as long as there is standing room at the front. The area under a dormer can be a good place for a sink.

Angles & corners

If the area is large enough, the best solution for an awkward space is to build out from the wall to create a regular space within an irregular one. Otherwise, you may need to accommodate angles with angled fixtures, such as offset corner sinks and bathtubs. Toilets which are designed to fit into corners are also available, as are interlocking bath and shower cubicles.

Narrow spaces

The best layout for narrow locations aligns fixtures along one wall so that there is a clear route through the space. This ensures that plumbing runs remain simple, which also helps to keep the bathroom looking neater. Wall-hung toilets, bidets and sinks enhance the sense of space. Make sure you arrange the layout so there is some separation between the toilet and the bathtub; using a half-height partition will not block light. Top lighting in the form of skylights can help to counteract the lack of breadth.

LEFT: A FREESTANDING BATHTUB IS POSITIONED UNDER THE EAVES IN A CONVERTED ATTIC. A ROOFLIGHT FLOODS THE BATHROOM WITH NATURAL LIGHT.

RIGHT: HERE, THE BATHTUB OCCUPIES THE CENTRE OF THE LAYOUT AND THE AREA UNDER THE EAVES HAS BEEN DEVOTED TO STORAGE SPACE.

Wet rooms

Wet rooms have become increasingly popular in recent years and are an ideal solution if you are short of space. They also have a rather elemental quality, which can be very appealing. In a wet room, all surfaces are fully waterproofed and the shower drains directly into the floor. If you have enough room, you can also include a bathtub. It is less easy, however, to incorporate much in the way of storage.

- The floor must be laid so that water flows into the drain and does not remain on the surface.
- The underlying structure must be professionally waterproofed, either with an impermeable membrane or a bituminous layer. Make sure that you employ someone who has experience in this type of work.
- Walls and floors must be made of waterproof materials. Flooring should be non-slip.
- All light fittings should be fully enclosed in waterproof housings.
- For greater comfort, think about installing underfloor heating. Again, you will need a qualified professional to carry out the work.
- You can enhance the sense of space by opting for wall-hung fittings and wall-mounted fixtures. Wall-hung sinks and toilets keep the floor area clear. Wall-mounted taps and shower heads are visually neat.

ABOVE: THIS WET ROOM FEATURES THREE TYPES OF SHOWER: FOOT, HAND-HELD AND FULL-HEIGHT. ALL DRAIN INTO THE TEAK SLATTED FLOOR.

LEFT: WET ROOMS ARE AT THEIR MOST ELEMENTAL WHEN DETAILING IS MINIMAL. THIS SINK IS POSITIONED TO TAKE ADVANTAGE OF NATURAL LIGHT.

Home spas

There are two basic approaches to recreating the sensory experience and therapeutic benefits of a spa at home. One is to go the high-tech route and kit out your bathroom with special features such as hydrotherapy baths and showers. The other is to go back to basics and take inspiration from the bathing practices of other cultures, such as the rejuvenating cleansing offered by a sauna or steam room, or the deep relaxation derived from soaking in a Japanese hot tub or overflow bath. However, you will need considerable floor area and a good deal more in your budget.

- Large jacuzzis or whirlpool baths hold much more water than standard bathtubs, which means that the floor needs to be strong enough to bear the additional load.
- Steam rooms and saunas require additional servicing and specialist installation.
- Hydrotherapy baths and showers require high water pressure, which may need to be boosted with a pump.
- Some types of whirlpool bath need to be installed so that the underside remains accessible.
- Cheaper hydrotherapy baths and showers can be noisy.
- Japanese hot tubs need to be kept filled with water to prevent the wood from cracking.
- Many specialist fixtures consume more energy and water than standard fixtures.

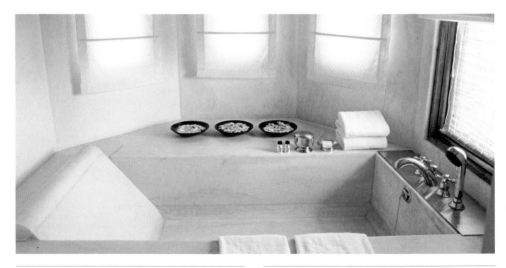

ABOVE: A SUNKEN BATH WITH A RECLINING BACKREST MAKES AN UNBEATABLE PLACE TO UNWIND. SOOTHING NATURAL LIGHT IS FILTERED THROUGH WINDOW BLINDS.

RIGHT: SCANDINAVIAN SAUNAS ARE AVAILABLE AS PREFABRICATED WOODEN CABINS OR THEY CAN BE CUSTOM-BUILT TO SUIT YOUR HOME.

Capsule bathrooms

Stand-alone or capsule bathrooms range from prefabricated shower cubicles to purpose-built pods or modules enclosing sinks, bathtubs, showers and toilets. Essentially a way of incorporating a bathroom within a larger area or open-plan space, the capsule bathroom emerged from the type of spatial planning used for converted lofts.

Shower cabinets

- The shower is enclosed within a single freestanding unit, which may be sited within a bedroom or wherever a servicing connection can be made.
- Walls, roof and floor can be moulded in one piece for total waterproofing.
- Transparent or opaline roofs dispel any sense of confinement.
- Up-market versions have spa features, such as massaging jets and steam settings.

Bathroom pods

- In a loft or open-plan area it often makes sense to group the kitchen and bathroom in a service core. Try to position a pod where it will not create dead space.
- Boxy enclosures are simpler and cheaper to construct, but curved shapes are more sculptural and are ideal for housing showers.
- Freestanding designs generally work best where there is plenty of head height. In a double-height loft, a bathroom pod will not stop the space from reading as a whole.
- Incorporating panels of frosted glass, Perspex and glass brick preserves privacy while creating a lighter and less dominant effect.

ABOVE: A SLIDING GLAZED SCREEN SEPARATES A MOSAIC-TILED CAPSULE BATHROOM FROM THE REST OF THE OPEN-PLAN SPACE.

LEFT: A CURVED BATHROOM POD IS ENCLOSED IN COLOURED PERSPEX PANELS THAT ALLOW LIGHT THROUGH BUT PRESERVE PRIVACY.

Outdoor bathing

The experience of showering or bathing outside need not be restricted to those living in warm climates. A shower can be rigged up in a garden to take advantage of fine weather; a sunken hot tub on a terrace is a delicious way to relax. Siting a bathroom where there is a close connection to a garden brings an elemental contact with nature that can be very restorative.

- Rooftop or ground-level locations offer the greatest opportunity for merging bathing areas with the world outside.
- If you are installing a shower or bathtub on a roof terrace, make sure the structure can bear the weight and that such a construction falls within permitted development. Showers and bathtubs must be adequately drained and surrounding areas fully waterproofed.
- Sliding or folding glass doors that can be fully opened allow air and light to circulate.
- If privacy is an issue, use frosted or etched glass, or glass bricks at the lower levels, and screen views from neighbouring houses or gardens with trellis, fencing or planting.
- Top lighting is very invigorating. A skylight placed over a shower or bath enhances the sense of wellbeing.
- Extend similar flooring materials indoors and out to blur the boundaries between the two.

ABOVE: SIMPLE OUTDOOR SHOWERS CAN BE VERY INVIGORATING, ESPECIALLY IN HOT CLIMATES OR SEASIDE AREAS.

RIGHT: HERE, A CUSTOM-BUILT GLASS-SIDED BATHTUB IS SITED BESIDE A HINGED WINDOW THAT OPENS ONTO A ROOF TERRACE.

Saving water

Water is a precious resource and must not be treated as if it were in limitless supply. In many parts of the world, legislation has been framed to help reduce domestic consumption.

- Fix all dripping taps and other leaks. Leaks are pure wastage. If you have a water meter, one way of checking whether you have a leak is to shut off the water and take two readings a few minutes apart. If they differ, you probably have a leak somewhere.
- Install a low-flush toilet. Alternatively, reduce the flush in a standard toilet by displacing water in the cistern using a water-saving device or a plastic bottle filled with pebbles.
- Use flow regulators on taps and showerheads. Various designs are available; some aerate the flow to cut the amount of water.
- Shower rather than bathe. If you have a power shower, which consumes much more water than a standard shower, limit yourself to showers of a few minutes or so.
- Do not leave the tap running while you wash your hands or clean your teeth. Running taps send 9 litres (16 pints) of clean water down the drain per minute.
- Run full loads in washing machines. When you need to buy a new appliance, choose one that has a water-saving programme.
- Meter your water supply to make yourself more water-conscious.

ABOVE: AERATED SHOWERHEADS AND TAPS CONSUME LESS WATER THAN STANDARD FITTINGS.

LEFT: SHOWERS MAKE A BETTER WATER-SAVING OPTION THAN BATHS, PROVIDED YOU LIMIT THEIR DURATION TO A FEW MINUTES OR SO.

Safety

Bathrooms present various everyday hazards, many of which can be addressed in the design process. Special care needs to be taken where children or the elderly are using the bathroom.

- Reduce the risk of slipping in the bathtub or shower by choosing trays with integral non-slip surfaces. Alternatively, use a non-slip rubber or slatted wooden mat.
- Certain types of flooring are more slippery than others. If you opt for a smooth flooring material, provide extra grip underfoot with a textured bathmat.
- Rounded corners, recessed taps and other fixtures help to prevent the risk of injury on a sharp edge.
- Thermostatic shower controls allow the water temperature to be preset and reduce the risk of accidental scalding.
- Water must never be allowed to come into contact with electricity: the combination is lethal. Very strict regulations govern bathroom wiring. Any alteration to existing wiring must be carried out by a qualified electrician.
- In the United Kingdom, only low-voltage shaver sockets are permissible in a bathroom. Lights must be either controlled by pull-cords inside the bathroom or switches outside. Laundry appliances and metal bathtubs must be earthed.
- In the United States, electrical sockets are permissible inside the bathroom provided they are at least 1.5m (5ft) away from the bathtub and are positioned high up the wall.
- If using bath oils in the bathtub or shower, be careful as they can leave the surfaces slippery.

ABOVE: WATERPROOF LIGHT FITTINGS SPECIFICALLY DESIGNED FOR BATHROOM USE PREVENT THE RISK OF WATER COMING INTO CONTACT WITH ELECTRICITY.

RIGHT: A RIDGED MAT PROVIDES EXTRA GRIP UNDERFOOT NEXT TO A BATHTUB. PAINTED WOOD CLADDING PROTECTS THE WALL AND ENCLOSES THE SIDE OF THE BATH.

Basic considerations

Bathroom fixtures and fittings have dramatically changed in recent years, with a host of new materials, designs and features coming onto the market, from custom-made bathtubs and sinks in marble, stone and wood, to exclusive ranges created by leading architects and designers. Mass retailers also stock a much greater variety of fittings than they used to, which means that there is ample choice whatever your budget.

Before you make your choice, take time to visit showrooms to see what is on offer. A fixture is a permanent feature and often a considerable investment may be entailed. Choosing the right bathroom fittings is not simply about making sure they fit into the space you have at your disposal, it is also about making sure that they suit your own physical framework: bathtubs must be long and deep enough, sinks and toilets should be a comfortable height.

- It is important to take into account the weight of the fixtures you are planning to install. Some materials are much heavier than others: a cast-iron bathtub, for example, can impose a significant additional load on the floor.
- Think long-term when you are making decisions about colour. Bear in mind that you might tire of a coloured bathroom range before it needs replacement. White is still the most popular choice.
- Consider how much aftercare is required. Certain materials, such as glass and metal, are more demanding in terms of upkeep.

ABOVE: CONTEMPORARY BATHROOM FITTINGS VARY WIDELY IN STYLE AND MATERIAL. THIS CLEAN-LINED DOUBLE SINK IS FITTED WITH MONOBLOCK MIXER TAPS.

LEFT: A HALF-PEDESTAL WALL-HUNG SINK OFFERS SOME LATITUDE WITH REGARD TO POSITIONING.

Bathtubs

Although it is generally a good idea to coordinate the design of bathroom fittings, the bathtub is one element that can be selected individually.

Practical considerations

Do not be afraid to try out different bathtubs to see which one feels the most comfortable. Lean back to see if there is enough support for your neck. Bathtubs should be long enough for you to stretch out fully, but not so long that you cannot brace your feet against the end. Vey deep bathtubs may be awkward if you like to read while soaking or if you need to bathe small children. Double-ended bathtubs allow two people to bathe comfortably. Contoured or reclining interiors limit you to one position.

- Different sizes and shapes of bathtub are available to accommodate different layouts, including corner and tapering bathtubs.
- Large or deep bathtubs consume more water than those of standard sizes, as do overflow or infinity edge styles.
- Cast-iron and stone bathtubs are very heavy. If you wish to install one, you may need to strengthen the floor. Acrylic bathtubs are much lighter and, if you want a large bathtub, may be the only choice, once you have taken into account the weight of you and the water when the bathtub is full.
- Find out whether the bathtub comes with tap holes already drilled or if you have the choice of where these can be mounted.

ABOVE: A CAST-IRON BATHTUB TRADITIONALLY HAS A ROLL-TOP EDGE AND DECORATIVE METAL FEET.

RIGHT: A LARGE SCULPTURAL BATHTUB IS PARTNERED BY A FLOOR-STANDING BATH FILLER.

continued

Bathtubs

Materials

- **Cast iron** Bathtubs made of enamel-coated cast iron are durable, scratchproof and stain-resistant. Several layers of porcelain enamel are fused onto a cast-iron shell to give a smooth glossy interior. Cast-iron bathtubs retain heat well and bathwater stays warm for longer. However, they are very heavy and can be difficult to install: usually a floor will need to be strengthened to bear the weight. Classic freestanding designs have roll-top edges and may be supported by decorative feet or shaped wooden blocks. Original reclaimed bathtubs are available from second-hand sources and can easily be refurbished. They come in single- or double-ended versions. A cast-iron bathtub can be a substantial investment.

- **Pressed steel** Steel is cheaper and lighter than cast-iron. It comes in a wide variety of shapes, sizes, colours and designs. Shower bathtubs have flat bases and are wider at the shower end.

- **Acrylic** A very light material, acrylic can be produced in a wide range of sizes and shapes, including offset and circular designs. It is more hygienic than other materials, easy to clean and repair if scratched, warm and non-slip. Quality and price vary widely: the best acrylic bathtubs are reinforced with fibreglass.

- **Stone** Although beautiful to look at, stone is incredibly heavy and does not retain heat well. Stone bathtubs are very expensive, especially when carved from solid blocks. Circular, sculptural shapes are most common. Artificial stone baths or those made of panels or slabs are cheaper and lighter.

- **Wood** Cedar and teak are naturally waterproof and are the types of wood most commonly used for bathtubs. Wood is an ideal material because of its tactile nature and high insulating properties. The Japanese hot tub – a deep short bathtub that is designed for sitting and soaking in rather than for washing – is one of the most typical designs. (The Japanese tend to wash themselves in a shower first.)

ABOVE: SOME TYPES OF PRESSED-STEEL BATHTUBS ARE DESIGNED TO BE INSET OR ENCLOSED BY PANELLING.

LEFT: THE EXTERIOR OF CAST-IRON BATHTUBS CAN BE PAINTED TO MATCH THE DÉCOR. THIS MODERN VERSION IS SUPPORTED ON WOODEN BLOCKS.

Sinks

Nowadays, sinks come in a huge range of types, sizes, shapes and materials, from tiny corner sinks suitable for cloakrooms to sculptural glass or stone vessels that make stunning focal points.

- Think about the functions you need the sink to fulfil. Does it need to be big enough for you to handwash delicate articles of clothing? How often will it be used? Will it be shared or would double sinks be a better option?
- Shaped or corner sinks are now available for awkward layouts.
- Most sinks are pre-drilled with tap holes, with the exception of freestanding or vessel sinks.
- Vitreous china, which is hygienic, durable and easy to clean, is the standard material, and the colour range is vast.
- The best glass sinks are finished with a silicone coating that makes them easier to keep clean. They are not suited to heavy use.
- Stone and wooden sinks introduce an element of tactility.
- Stainless steel sinks, which are damage-proof, have a utilitarian quality. Water-spotting can be a problem. Steel sinks with a brushed, matt finish are the easiest types to maintain.
- Cheaper wooden sinks and troughs are made of stained marine plyboard. The best wooden sinks are made of teak and are sometimes used for dishwashing in restaurants and hotels.

ABOVE: A STONE VESSEL SINK HAS A CERTAIN PURITY OF DESIGN. TAPS USUALLY HAVE TO BE FITTED EITHER BEHIND OR ABOVE THIS TYPE OF SINK.

RIGHT: THIS PLAIN, SQUARE VESSEL SINK IN VITREOUS CHINA HAS A UTILITARIAN RETRO FEEL.

continued

Sinks

Types of sink

- The pedestal sink, which is designed to conceal pipework, may be a separate element or part of a monoblock design. A pedestal sink is a dominant feature and it is best to choose a toilet from the same range. Pedestals are set at a standard height of between 850 and 900mm (33 and 35in).

- Half-pedestal wall-hung sinks have siphon covers to conceal pipework. They offer some latitude in terms of positioning, as they can be set at different heights.

- Inset sinks are one of the most common types of sink. They are designed to be dropped into a countertop or washstand, with only the top edge proud of the surface. Semi-inset sinks project slightly from the front. Underbowls are fixed directly under the top of a washstand or surround.

- Vessel sinks take the form of minimal, sculptural bowls that either sit on a counter or similar surface, or are suspended from wall-mounted brackets. Taps generally have to be fitted behind or on the wall above, and need to be positioned so that water drains directly into the waste, otherwise there will be a risk of splashing.

- Bespoke sinks can be commissioned from specialist contractors or suppliers in different formats, sizes and materials. A long shallow trough fitted with several taps, for example, can provide a neater solution than double sinks in a family or shared bathroom.

ABOVE: GLASS SINKS HAVE A SIMPLE, ELEMENTAL QUALITY. THEY ARE USUALLY COATED WITH SILICONE TO MAKE THEM EASIER TO CLEAN.

LEFT: TRADITIONAL OR RETRO-STYLE PEDESTAL SINKS CAN EITHER BE BOUGHT NEW OR SOURCED FROM AN ARCHITECTURAL SALVAGE YARD.

Toilets & bidets

Most toilets and bidets are made of porcelain or vitreous china. If space is tight, the bidet is one bathroom fixture that is likely to be omitted from the layout. Toilets and bidets should come from the same range and be sited close together.

- Standard toilets consist of a floor-mounted pan connected to a low-level cistern by a short flush pipe. The pan sits in front of the cistern (which takes up more floor area than the old-fashioned toilet with a high-level cistern, where the pan was sited directly underneath).
- Close-coupled toilets have cisterns that are directly attached to the pan.
- Back-to-the-wall toilets are floor-mounted and are supported either by a foot or a pedestal. They require concealed cisterns.
- Wall-hung toilets are suspended from the wall, which must be strong enough to bear the weight. The cistern is concealed behind a dummy panel.
- Corner toilets are available for difficult layouts.
- New low-flush toilets are highly efficient and consume very little water. Dual-flush toilets, which allow you to choose between a short flush and a full one, are also water-saving.
- If your water pressure is not sufficiently high, you may need to incorporate a low pressure valve with some types of toilet.

ABOVE: WALL-HUNG TOILETS LOOK NEAT AND CONTEMPORARY. WITH MORE FLOOR SURFACE VISIBLE UNDERNEATH, THEY CAN CREATE AN ILLUSION OF SPACE IN SMALLER BATHROOMS.

RIGHT: FOR VISUAL CONSISTENCY, TOILETS AND BIDETS SHOULD COME FROM THE SAME RANGE. THESE BLEND DISCREETLY INTO AN ALL-WHITE BATHROOM.

Showers

Showers are an eco-friendly alternative to bathing, saving both water and energy. The type of shower you can install will depend on your existing water system.

Water pressure

In most parts of the world, where water supply is direct, water pressure will be sufficiently high for showering wherever the shower is located. In Britain, where most households have an indirect supply, the storage cistern needs to be at least 3–4m (10–13ft) above the showerhead. The alternative is to convert to a direct supply or to install a pump. However, pumps cannot be installed if you have a combination boiler and no hot-water cylinder. You may need advice from a shower installer or plumber.

Enclosures

- Over-the-bath showers are the simplest and most common option and can be enclosed by a rigid bath screen or shower curtain.
- Shower doors and enclosures are usually made of toughened safety glass. Doors may be hinged, pivoting or sliding. Frameless shower doors have a neat, minimal look.
- Stand-alone shower cubicles are often constructed in one piece for maximum waterproofing.
- Trays come in different materials: ceramic trays are very strong; acrylic trays are less stable than ceramic varieties; enamelled steel can be slippery; stone or hardwood trays can be commissioned from specialists.

ABOVE: WATER FROM A POWERFUL 'RAIN' SHOWERHEAD DRAINS THROUGH A GRIDDED TEAK FLOOR.

LEFT: A WALK-IN MARBLE SHOWER IS MINIMALLY SCREENED FROM THE REST OF THE BEDROOM BY A FRAMELESS GLASS PANEL.

continued

Showers

ABOVE: A CORNER SHOWER FEATURES AN ADJUSTABLE
SHOWERHEAD AND A CERAMIC TRAY.

RIGHT: A LUXURIOUS DOUBLE SHOWER INCLUDES A
SEPARATE HAND-HELD SHOWER AND RECESSED AND
CONCEALED LIGHTING.

Showerheads

In Britain, where water pressure is low, showerheads have traditionally taken the form of large watering-can roses to deliver enough water. American or European-style heads, which deliver finer sprays, may need to be pump-assisted if you have an indirect water system.

- Adjustable showerheads allow you to choose the type of spray you want, from needle-fine to full power.
- Fixed showerheads are attached to a shower arm or fixed to the wall.
- Flexible showerheads have hoses and are attached to a bar so you can vary the height.
- 'Rain' showerheads are over-scaled to simulate the effect of standing in a downpour.
- Side jets and vertical rain bars, which direct water at the body for a massaging effect, are also available.

Controls

- Bath-shower mixers and hand-held shower sets are controlled by diverters, which direct water either to the shower or the main taps. Abrupt temperature change can be a problem and is often the result of variations in pressure between hot and cold water. To prevent this, hot water connections should be made close to the hot-water cylinder.
- The simplest controls regulate temperature only, using a lever or disc.
- Dual-control thermostatic valves allow you to preset the temperature before getting into the shower and vary the water flow.
- Some controls have child-safety devices.

Taps

As mentioned previously, in Britain water pressure is often low. Here, taps need to have larger bores to deliver water fast enough to fill a bathtub or sink. In other countries, taps are more elegant and minimal. If you want to use an American or European tap fitting in Britain, you will probably need a pump unless you have a direct water supply.

- Make sure the taps fit the sanitaryware and choose a style that is in keeping with the style of your sink or bathtub.
- Wall- or surface-mounted spouts or taps should be positioned so that they send water directly down the plughole. They allow the sculptural lines of a sink or freestanding bathtub to be uninterrupted.
- Think about maintenance. Stainless steel and chrome- or nickel-plated cast brass taps are easy to keep clean. Brass-plated taps require frequent polishing.
- Sink taps vary from separate pillar taps for hot and cold, mixer taps where separate valves control the temperatures, and monoblock mixers, which are fitted to a single tap hole.
- For bathtubs, it is preferable to have a single filler that mixes hot and cold water before it comes out of the spout. In some designs, the valves are separate from the spout, which allows freedom of position.

ABOVE: A WALL-MOUNTED TAP WITH A SINGLE LEVER CONTROL IS SIMPLE AND UNFUSSY.

LEFT: AN ELEGANTLY CURVED MIXER TAP CAN BE SWIVELLED FROM SIDE TO SIDE. THIS MODERN DESIGN REQUIRES THREE TAP HOLES.

Special fixtures

At the upper end of the market, there is a wide range of special fittings and fixtures that enable you to recreate a spa experience at home. Hydrotherapy baths and showers aid relaxation and can deliver other therapeutic benefits, too, especially for those with back, muscular or circulation problems.

- Spa bathtubs feature small jets at the bottom which release tiny bubbles of warmed air into the water. The effect is gentle and soothing.
- Whirlpool bathtubs have a massaging effect. A pump underneath forces water or water mixed with air through jets at the side, the strength of which can be controlled. The effect is enhanced in bigger bathtubs where there is more room for the water to circulate.
- 'Waterfalls' feature jets behind the headrest to massage the neck. Top-of-the-range models use ultrasound in combination with the jets.
- Similar hydrotherapy features are available in showers: vertical and back jets provide a massaging effect, adjustable showerheads produce a range of effects from cascades or waterfalls to fine needle spray, and some showers have special aromatherapy jets for dispersing scented water.
- Chromatherapy baths and showers incorporate LEDs, or light emitting diodes, to add the dimension of colour to the bathing or showering experience.

ABOVE: THIS OVERFLOW BATHTUB IN SWEDISH LIMESTONE HAS GROOVED CHANNELS AT THE SIDE WHERE WATER TRICKLES AWAY.

RIGHT: OVER-SCALED, ADJUSTABLE SHOWERHEADS ALLOW YOU TO VARY THE EFFECT, FROM FINE MASSAGING JETS TO TROPICAL-STYLE DOWNPOURS.

Lighting

All bathrooms, however small they are, need a combination of different types of light. Bright task lighting around a mirror, can be angled and positioned so that your face is evenly, but not harshly, illuminated. In addition, you may require a softer background light to create a pleasant relaxing atmosphere, especially if you regularly enjoy soaking in the bathtub.

Natural light is a bonus, but if your bathroom lacks windows, you may be able to introduce it by 'borrowing' light from adjacent areas via glazed screens or doors. Top lighting from a high-level window or skylight can also be hugely invigorating.

Safety considerations

With bathroom lighting, practicality is the most important issue. Water and electricity are a dangerous combination and the bathroom is where the two come into closest proximity. It is essential to choose fittings specifically designed for bathroom use and to consult a qualified electrician when planning a scheme. Regulations vary from country to country.

Bathroom lighting tends to be fitted, which means that once the lights are installed you will not be able to change them easily. Plan the lighting once you have established where the main fittings and fixtures will go.

LEFT: LIGHTING CONCEALED UNDERNEATH WALL UNITS ILLUMINATES A PAIR OF SINKS, WHILE UNDERLIGHTING MAKES THE FITTED BASE UNITS APPEAR TO FLOAT.

ABOVE: DISCREET SIDE- AND UPLIGHTING ACCENTUATES THE FORM OF THIS BATHTUB AND CREATES A GENTLE AND RELAXING BACKGROUND LIGHT.

continued

Lighting

Task lighting

The area around the sink and mirror is where you need the brightest light for shaving and applying make-up. It should not be harsh, but it does need to be bright enough for you to see what you are doing. The position of task light is all-important. Bright light shining down from above will cast heavy shadows on the face. It is better to light the mirror from both sides, using small bulbs or vertical tubes. Alternately, balance top lighting with a pair of wall-mounted lights to either side of the sink. Some bathroom mirrors or mirrored cabinets also have integral lights.

Background lighting

When the bathroom was treated more as a functional area than a room in its own right, a single overhead light fixture was the standard solution. Try to avoid this if at all possible – a single light source has a deadening effect and can create glare, especially in an area where there are many reflective surfaces and finishes. Multiple points of light, such as recessed downlights, are much more atmospheric and space-enhancing. Wall-mounted uplights bounce light off the ceiling; concealed lights reduce the impact of bulky fixtures. Some bathtubs and sinks incorporate backlit translucent panels that create an evocative glow. Even more magical is water lit by fibre optics, a feature of many hydrotherapy baths and showers.

ABOVE: A COMBINATION OF RECESSED DOWNLIGHTS AND CONCEALED LIGHTING UNDER THE COUNTER CREATES A CALM AMBIENCE AND HIGHLIGHTS THE GLASS SINK.

RIGHT: THE BEST WAY TO LIGHT A MIRROR IS FROM EITHER SIDE, USING SMALL BULBS OR VERTICAL TUBES.

Heating

All bathrooms, no matter how small, need some form of heating to provide a comfortable environment. You will need a qualified plumber or electrician to carry out the installation.

Underfloor heating

- This is ideal for use under inherently cold, dense materials such as stone, tile or concrete. These materials have a high thermal mass, so they gain heat slowly and also release it slowly.
- Discreet and space-saving, underfloor heating is an asset in smaller bathrooms.
- Underfloor heating using hot water needs more subfloor depth than electrical mat installations.
- Temperature can be set at a low background level to save energy.

Conventional radiators

- Traditionall radiators can be run off an existing heating system.
- They are best for larger rooms, where there is more floor area.
- Wall-hung or vertical radiators maximize space and are available in various formats.
- Equally space-saving, slim panel radiators can be recessed into the wall.

Heated towel rails

- In a very small bathroom, a heated towel rail can supply enough heat to make the room comfortable.
- Different finishes and designs allow you to coordinate the towel rail with taps and other bathroom fittings.
- Most heated towel rails can be connected to an existing heating system. Oil-filled rails are also available.
- Some towel rails incorporate an electrical element in the bottom rail so you can use them in the summer when the heating is off.

ABOVE: A RETRO-STYLE RADIATOR IS TUCKED UNDER THE BROAD WOOD COUNTER THAT SUPPORTS THE SINK.

LEFT: HEATED TOWEL RAILS COME IN A WIDE RANGE OF SIZES AND DESIGNS. MOST CONNECT TO THE EXISTING HEATING SYSTEM.

Storage

Most bathrooms are essentially fitted spaces, so you need to consider storage right from the outset. The smaller the space at your disposal, the more ruthless you need to be about what possessions you keep there.

- Do not keep anything in the bathroom that is not in daily use or directly relevant to what takes place there.
- Unless you have plenty of room, do not store bulk supplies of toilet paper in the bathroom. The same goes for bath linen.
- Possessions to keep out on view or close at hand include: toothbrushes and toothpaste, soaps and other grooming products, fresh towels and toilet paper. Cleaning products also need to be readily accessible, preferably hidden in concealed storage.
- Most people like to keep medicines and home remedies in the bathroom, although some medicines deteriorate more quickly in hot, steamy conditions. If there are children in the household, make sure that prescription medicines, other remedies and cleaning products are stored out of reach, preferably in a locked cabinet. Do not lock a first aid box because you need to be able to access it at a moment's notice.
- Periodically weed out old cosmetics and beauty products. Many of these have a shelf life of only six months or so.

ABOVE: A STORAGE CUPBOARD IS TUCKED UNDER THE EAVES AND CONCEALED BY WOOD PANELLING.

RIGHT: LARGE MIRRORED WALL-HUNG CABINETS KEEP PRODUCTS, COSMETICS AND ACCESSORIES OUT OF VIEW.

continued

Storage

Types of storage

- Built-in storage in the bathroom allows you to conceal plumbing runs, toilet cisterns and the undersides of sinks, while integrating separate fixtures into a well-considered whole. In a small bathroom, the effect can be to increase the sense of space, even though there will be some sacrifice of floor area.

- Washstands, which support the sink, come in a wide range of sizes, styles and materials. Some can be wall-hung, which is visually neat.

- Wall units can be used to house bathroom clutter. These do not have to be very deep as most of the items that need to be stored in a bathroom can be kept on narrow shelves.

- If you have plenty of floor area, freestanding furniture, such as chests and armoires, can fulfil the bulk of your storage needs.

- Glass shelving is a good way of storing bathroom supplies: because it is transparent, it does not intrude visually and if products leak or spill, it is easy to clean up. Upstanding chrome or metal rails prevent bottles sliding off and smashing.

- Containers of various descriptions – boxes, baskets, and bags – are useful for storing like with like or providing dedicated storage for different members of the household.

- Mobile trolleys can be used as convenient places to keep bath products and towels near to the bathtub.

ABOVE: WALL-HUNG WASHSTANDS LEAVE THE FLOOR AREA CLEAR, PROVIDING ADDITIONAL SPACE FOR FITTED OR FREESTANDING STORAGE.

LEFT: IN A FULLY FITTED BATHROOMS IN-BUILT NICHES ARE USEFUL PLACES TO STORE TOILET ROLLS AND BATHROOM PRODUCTS.

INTRODUCTION
PLANNING & LAYOUT
FIXTURES & FITTINGS
DECOR & DETAIL

Basic considerations

Practicality is a key issue when it comes to devising a decorative scheme for a bathroom. Surfaces and finishes need to be as water-resistant as possible, which means selecting appropriate materials and ensuring all joints and seams are tight and fully sealed so that damp cannot penetrate.

There remains plenty of scope, however, for expressing your tastes and preferences through colour, pattern and texture. In many cases, all three elements will be combined in a particular choice of material.

- Size is an important factor when considering bathroom design. Small areas can only take a limited amount of strong colour or pattern. Single colour schemes can be a very effective way of making a small space seem larger.
- Larger areas can accommodate more obvious changes in tone, scale and material because there is more breathing space.
- Think about the quality of the natural light, along with how much daylight the room receives. A bathroom that faces north (in the northern hemisphere) will have a whiter, chillier light than one that faces south or west.
- Decorative make-overs can be a good way of giving a tired bathroom a facelift, provided basic fixtures and fittings are in sound condition. In a small bathroom, you will be able to afford better quality materials because the surface area is more limited.

ABOVE: THE HARDWOOD PANELLED DOORS OF THESE STORAGE CUPBOARDS PROVIDE DEPTH OF CHARACTER AND TEXTURAL INTEREST.

LEFT: A WALL COMPLETELY TILED IN RED MOSAIC MAKES AN EFFECTIVE CONTRAST TO THE NEUTRAL TONE OF THE STONE CLADDING.

Colour

Colour is hugely evocative and different shades can create either an uplifting or a soothing effect. In relatively small areas, which many bathrooms are, it packs a powerful punch. Think about the quality of light. Rooms that face north or east need colours from the warmer end of the spectrum; cool colours, such as blues, suit sunnier rooms.

- White has strong connotations of purity and cleanliness and is the default bathroom colour. It is a good choice for basic fittings and fixtures: coloured suites can be very dominant and you may tire of the shade before you can afford to replace the fittings. In the right context, where there is good natural light, an all white décor is luxurious and restful.
- Blue is another popular bathroom colour, due to its natural association with water, and is generally calm and soothing. Avoid chilly blues, such as blue-grey, where natural light levels are low.
- Warm colours such as reds and oranges are energizing. In a small bathroom, they can be a little dominant and are best restricted to accent shades. Otherwise, they need plenty of breathing space.
- Earth colours such as neutral shades of biscuit, terracotta, cream, brown and off-white go well with natural surfaces and materials, such as wood and stone.
- Edgy colours that include both warm and cool tones, such as *eau de nil*, aquamarine and lavender vary according to light conditions. The resulting ambiguity is a good way of generating mood and atmosphere.

ABOVE: A SINGLE WALL PICKED OUT IN BRIGHT RED ADDS A TOUCH OF VIBRANCY TO A SMALL BATHROOM.

RIGHT: GREEN IS AN INHERENTLY RESTFUL COLOUR AND WORKS WELL IN AREAS THAT RECEIVE A GOOD QUALITY OF NATURAL LIGHT.

Pattern & texture

Pattern

From the subtle to the more overt, pattern can
be introduced into bathrooms in all sorts of
ways. Bear in mind that in small spaces large-
scale repeats can be very attention-seeking and
overly dominant, all the more so if they are
figurative. If space is limited, the best option can
be to use pattern to define an area, such as a
contrasting border or banding of tilework, or to
provide a sense of rhythm that breaks up a
uniform surface. In this respect, even a grid of
tiles or a patchwork of randomly coloured mosaic
constitutes a sort of pattern. Another option is to
restrict pattern to the floor, where it is less
insistent. On the walls, pattern is much more
enclosing. Like colour, pattern can also be used
as an accent. Patterned towels, shower curtains
and other accessories are easy to change when
you get tired of them.

Texture

Closely allied to pattern is texture and, in the
case of many natural materials, the two are
virtually indistinguishable. The variations in
texture that arise when you combine different
materials, such as a wooden washstand with
stone flooring, provide interest and depth of
character in plain or neutral schemes.

ABOVE: MOSAIC TILES BRING BOTH PATTERN AND
TEXTURE INTO THE BATHROOM. THEY ARE AVAILABLE
IN SHEET FORM AND COME IN SINGLE-COLOURS,
GEOMETRIC DESIGNS OR RANDOMLY PATTERNED
SELECTIONS, AS HERE.

LEFT: SLATE TILES, IN A DEEP BROWN, CLAD THE WALLS
AND SIDES OF A BATHTUB. THE SURFACE TEXTURE
CREATES AN APPEALINGLY TACTILE ENVIRONMENT.

Wall treatments

All bathrooms, however well they are ventilated, are prone to condensation. Where layouts are compact, there is also a high probability that walls will get splashed from time to time. If not fully waterproof, bathroom surfaces and finishes should be highly water-resistant.

- Good preparation is essential if you are going to clad or tile walls. If the underlying surface is not even, tilework will be an irregular eyesore. It is worth getting battered walls replastered to create a professional finish.
- Try to find natural breaks between different types of wall treatment or extend the same material all the way up the wall. A meagre bit of tiling around the bath or sink looks skimpy.
- In a small space, using the same material on the walls as the floor can be a good way of providing visual unity. Many materials, including ceramic tile and stone, are available in floor and wall formats, with wall tiles being thinner and lighter in weight.
- It is a good idea to get professional help with installation, particularly if you are opting for expensive or unwieldy materials.
- Think about maintenance. Expanses of sheet glass or metal have a cutting-edge aesthetic, but are harder to keep pristine.

ABOVE: STAINED WOOD PANELLING LAID HORIZONTALLY EMPHASIZES THE LENGTH OF THIS BATHROOM.

RIGHT: STANDARD TONGUE-AND-GROOVE PANELLING, PAINTED WHITE, HAS A REFRESHING SIMPLICITY.

continued

Wall treatments

Materials

- **Paint** A simple, affordable treatment for walls and ceilings not immediately adjacent to wet areas, paint provides a quick cover-up. Choose paints specially formulated for bathroom use, which contain vinyl and may also include a fungicide to prevent the growth of mould.

- **Paper** Choose paper specially designed for bathroom use which has a vinyl coating to improve water resistance. Do not use paper in wet or steamy areas, where it will be more likely to lift and peel away.

- **Wood** Cladding made of wood gives a bathroom a snug, tactile quality. Painted tongue-and-groove softwood panelling is a popular choice and readily available. Sheets of marine ply, where the layers are bonded with waterproof glue, is another economic option. Hardwoods such as cedar and teak are naturally water-resistant, but must come from sustainable sources.

- **Tiling** Ceramic tiles are durable, easy to handle, readily available and come in a huge range of sizes, finishes, colours and designs. The most common formats are 100mm (4in) and 150mm (6in) squares; rectangular 'metro' versions and hexagonal tiles are also available. Porcelain tiles have a contemporary edge and are generally more expensive than ceramic. Stone tiles are at the upper end of the price range. Small tiles can be stuck with adhesive; larger formats require steel fixings. Protective dressings are advisable to prevent staining. Mosaic is another popular bathroom choice, available in single-colour sheets or patterns.

ABOVE: THESE RETRO-STYLE CERAMIC TILES HAVE BEEN LAID IN STAGGERED ROWS. TILING LOOKS BEST WHEN IT IS TAKEN ALL THE WAY UP TO THE CEILING.

LEFT: THE SAME FORMAT STONE TILES USED FOR WALLS AND FLOORING GIVE A MODERN UNIFIED LOOK.

Flooring

Bathroom flooring must be waterproof. For this reason, carpets, rugs and natural-fibre coverings tend to be ruled out. In a small bathroom, sheet flooring is ideal; otherwise, it is essential to ensure that joints or seams are fully sealed to prevent damp from penetrating underneath.

Practical considerations

- How easy will it be to keep the floor clean? Are specialist seals or dressings required? Is the material you would like to use resistant to chemicals and stains?
- Any flooring material used in a wet room must be fully waterproof.
- Solid floors made of stone or tile can be chilly underfoot. For extra comfort, you might consider installing underfloor heating.
- Most solid, natural materials require specialist installation, which will add to the cost.
- Very heavy materials may need to be laid over a strengthened subfloor, particularly if the bathroom is located on an upper storey.
- However careful you are, it is hard to avoid wetting the bathroom floor from time to time. Smooth surfaces increase the risk of slipping. Consider using mosaic, studded rubber or textured tiles for better grip underfoot.
- In a small area, you might be able to afford a more expensive flooring material than you would elsewhere in the home.

ABOVE: FOR GREATER COMFORT, UNDERFLOOR HEATING CAN BE INSTALLED BENEATH STONE OR CERAMIC TILES.

RIGHT: A CLASSIC CHEQUERED TILE FLOOR IS BOTH AESTHETICALLY APPEALING AND PRACTICAL.

continued

Flooring

Materials

- **Wood** While warm and tactile underfoot, wood is susceptible to changes in humidity and adversely affected by repeated wetting, which means you need to be careful about the type you select and also its subsequent treatment. Cedar and teak are water-resistant hardwoods, and slatted teak floors are a particularly good choice for wet areas. You can paint and seal existing floorboards, and marine products such as yacht varnish provide the most protection.

- **Stone** A stone floor will bring a touch of class to your bathroom: marble, limestone, slate and travertine are all suitable and come in a wide range of colours and patterns. Tile sizes and formats vary. Choose a honed or sanded finish for better grip. Stone is heavy, so you may need to check that the existing subfloor can bear the weight. All stone flooring requires professional installation and most needs protective dressing to prevent staining.

- **Tile & mosaic** Choose matt-textured ceramic tiles to reduce slipperiness underfoot. Mosaic, because of its tight grid, also provides a good grip. Choose stone mosaic for flooring, rather than mosaic made of glass or polished marble.

- **Linoleum, vinyl, rubber & cork** These materials are all available in sheet or tile formats and come in a wide variety of colours. Linoleum is a natural, high-quality product that is warm, durable, anti-bacterial and resistant to acid and oil. Vinyl ranges from cheap to relatively expensive and will not raise the floor level when installed. Rubber flooring comes in studded or textured finishes to reduce the risk of slipping. Cork is resilient, warm and quiet.

ABOVE: HARDWOOD FLOORING BRINGS QUALITY TO A BATHROOM. IT NEEDS TO BE THOROUGHLY SEALED TO PROVIDE PROTECTION FROM WATER DAMAGE.

LEFT: WHITE HEXAGONAL TILING MAKES A PRACTICAL AND STYLISH BATHROOM FLOOR. SIMILAR DESIGNS ARE AVAILABLE IN SHEET FORM.

Mirrors

A mirror is not only an indispensable aid to grooming, it enhances natural light and dissolves spatial boundaries by multiplying views.

Sink mirrors

Mirrors are generally set above a sink, set at a height to facilitate shaving and applying make-up. There is a wide variety of shapes and sizes available, most of which are fixed to the wall with screws. For closer inspection, you can supplement a basic mirror with an enlarging mirror on an extendable or concertina arm. Mirrors do not have to be specifically designed for bathroom use. Antique or retro-style mirrors, available from junk shops or salvage yards, add decorative flair.

Mirrored cabinets

Wall-hung mirrored cabinets usefully combine two functions in one. Special features include folding side panels to enable you to see your face in profile, inset enlarging mirrors for close scrutiny, integral lights and heating or demisting elements to prevent condensation.

Sheet mirror

Large expanses of mirrored glass placed on facing walls enhance the sense of space and can be a particularly good way of making a small bathroom seem bigger, provided you feel comfortable with the added exposure. Mirror is heavy, however, and it will need secure wall anchorage. Mirrored surfaces also require more in the way of maintenance.

ABOVE: TWO LARGE EXPANSES OF SHEET MIRROR, FIXED TO THE WALLS OVER A BATHTUB AND STORAGE UNIT, MULTIPLY VIEWS AND ENHANCE THE SENSE OF SPACE.

RIGHT: A LARGE MIRROR IN A PERIOD FRAME PROPPED AGAINST THE WALL REFLECTS LIGHT IN AN OPEN-PLAN BEDROOM/BATHROOM.

Detail

In a bathroom, details embrace all those working elements – handles, towel rails and toilet-roll holders – that must operate properly for the space to function as a whole, as well accessories and decorative touches that contribute to a sense of wellbeing.

Window treatments

Natural light is a bonus in a bathroom and wherever possible windows should be minimally screened. Clean-lined treatments such as blinds are better than curtains, which trap moisture.

- Fabric blinds, such as Roman or roller blinds, are neat and tailored in appearance.
- Adjustable blinds in wood or metal, such as Venetian blinds and vertical louvres, allow you to vary the amount of light.
- Translucent screens made of Perspex provide privacy without blocking light.
- Replacing clear window glass with obscured, frosted or etched glass, screens the interior.

Doors

Changing a door or changing the way an existing door operates can make a lot of difference to your bathroom, especially if it lacks windows or is on the small side.

- If space is very tight, rehanging an existing door so that it opens outwards can make a layout more workable. Alternatively, you can replace a standard door with a sliding panel or a door that folds back on itself.
- Doors that have glazed panels allow light to filter through from adjacent areas, which is an asset if your bathroom is fully internal.
- If the bathroom door is a cheap hollow-core version, upgrading to a panelled or solid type adds a touch of quality.

RIGHT: COLOURFUL OR PATTERNED SHOWER CURTAINS ARE AN ECONOMICAL WAY OF ADDING VISUAL INTEREST AND CAN BE CHANGED EASILY WHEN YOU TIRE OF THEM.

LEFT: A SINGLE ROW OF ANTIQUE PATTERNED TILES ADDS DEFINITION TO AN ALL-WHITE CLOAKROOM.

continued

Detail

Washstands

Many of the materials suitable for flooring or wall cladding also make good tops for washstands. Stone can be cut to order to provide a seamless surface under which a sink can be mounted; alternatively, you can source good-quality offcuts from salvage yards and stonemasons. Wood makes an effective contrast if other surfaces and finishes are uniformly hard and smooth. Composite materials, such as Corian, are solid and self-coloured, and can be cut into any shape.

Bath linen & mats

As far as comfort is concerned, nothing is more important than what goes next to the skin. Choose the best bath linen you can afford; it will last longer and be a pleasure to use.

- Weave and fibre density are the two factors that determine the absorbency of a towel. Waffle weave and terry cloth are more absorbent than velvet pile.
- Natural fibres tend to feel best. All-cotton is a popular choice. Cotton/linen blends have a more exfoliating texture.
- Fabric mats with a non-slip backing are sensible if your bathroom floor is smooth. Cork mats or duckboard are good alternatives.

Small fittings

In a small bathroom, fittings are more visible, so opt for simple designs and restrict yourself to what is absolutely necessary. It is always a good idea to coordinate finishes and designs. Upgrading acrylic or ceramic fittings to chrome or brushed steel will impart a sense of quality.

ABOVE: A CHROME SOAP DISH IN A TRADITIONAL STYLE IS DESIGNED TO FIT ON THE RIM OF THE BATHTUB.

RIGHT: A WOODEN LADDER PROPPED AGAINST THE WALL IN FRONT OF A RADIATOR MAKES AN ELEGANT IMPROVISED TOWEL RAIL.

Display

Bathrooms are not the most obvious places for decorative display, but a few personal touches add to the mood of relaxation and make the space more liveable. It is often a good idea if what you put on display is also in regular use.

- Decanting bath salts and lotions into an array of glass bottles or attractive storage jars provides more visual pleasure than viewing the same products in their original packaging. Bath brushes, loofahs and natural sponges are also handsome enough to display.
- If you have enough wall space, framed photographs, prints and paintings add interest and charm. The frames must be watertight to prevent condensation penetrating behind the glass and ruining the picture. In a downstairs cloakroom or powder room, however, where conditions are not humid, you can collage the walls to your heart's content.
- Scent provides an additional dimension to the bathroom. Steer clear of synthetic fragrance or *pot pourri* and opt for aromatherapy oils or incense sticks. A few drops of oil can be gently heated in a diffuser to promote specific restorative benefits – lavender, for example, is calming and soothing. Special ceramic holders are available for burning incense sticks.
- Nothing can beat candles for creating a special mood. Flickering tea lights add a magical dimension to a long relaxing soak.

ABOVE: A BROAD SHELF AT THE TOP OF A DADO PANEL PROVIDES A PLACE TO DISPLAY FRAMED PICTURES AND OTHER DECORATIVE OBJECTS.

LEFT: AN ARRAY OF BLACK POTS MAKES A GRAPHIC CONTRAST TO A NEUTRAL-TONED DECORATIVE SCHEME.

Index

Acknowledgements

The publisher would like to thank Red Cover Picture Library for their kind permission to reproduce the following photographs:

2 James Mitchell; 6–7 Karyn Millet (Designer: Molly Isaksen, Landscape Design: Leland Walmsley of NWA); 10 Paul Ryan-Goff; 11 Mark York; 12 Andrew Wood; 13 Winfried Heinze; 16 Jake Fitzjones; 17 Ken Hayden; 18 Paul Ryan-Goff (Architect: Kastrup & Sjunnesson); 19 Niall McDiarmid; 20 Lucinda Symons; 21 Andrew Twort; 22 Patrick Spence; 23 Grant Govier (Designer: Luxuria); 24 Huntley Hedworth; 25 Paul Ryan-Goff (Architect: Kastrup & Sjunnesson); 26 James Mitchell; 27 Simon McBride; 28 Ken Hayden (www.amanresorts.com); 29 Warren Smith; 30 Ken Hayden; 31 Chris Tubbs; 32 Alun Callender; 33 Winfried Heinze; 34 Wayne Vincent; 35 Robin Matthews; 36 Johnny Bouchier; 37 Chris Tubbs (Architect: Honky, Designer: Honky Design); 38 Ed Reeve; 39 Huntley Hedworth; 40 Christopher Drake; 41 Debi Treloar (Interior Designer: Tanya Payne: P+P Interiors, www.shootspaces.com); 42 Ken Hayden; 43 Paul Ryan-Goff (Architect: Kastrup & Sjunnesson); 44 Henry Wilson; 45 James Silverman; 46 Tom Scott; 47 Paul Massey (Lloyd Davies of Manchester, supplied all the furniture, 'Northern Land' owners company); 48 Stuart McIntyre; 49 Henry Wilson; 50 N Minh & J Wass; 51 Warren Smith (Architect: Form Architecture); 52 Sasfi Hope-Ross (Architect: NBR Architects); 53 Brian Harrison; 56 Winfried Heinze (Designer: David Wallace); 57 Henry Wilson; 58 Christopher Drake; 59 Grant Govier (Designer: Luxuria); 60 Winfried Heinze; 61 Jake Fitzjones (Designer: Shani Zion); 62 Warren Smith; 63 Graham Atkins-Hughes; 64 Winfried Heinze; 65 Nick Carter; 66 Dan Duchars; 67 Alun Callender; 68 Jake Fitzjones (Designer: Rachel Harding); 69 Ed Reeve; 70 Jake Fitzjones; 71 Ed Reeve (Designer: Miranda Cahane); 72 Simon McBride; 73 Robin Matthews; 74 Paul Ryan-Goff (Architect: Kastrup & Sjunnesson); 75 Warren Smith (Designer: Mowlem & Co Kitchens, Stylist: Trudy Goodwin); 76 Warren Smith; 77 Ken Hayden; 78 Winfried Heinze; 79 Ken Hayden; 80 Winfried Heinze; 81 Ken Hayden; 82 Niall McDiarmid; 83 Henry Wilson; 84 Jake Fitzjones; 85 Warren Smith; 88 Ed Reeve (Designers: Who Designs); 89 Jake Fitzjones; 90 Jake Fitzjones; 91 Graham Atkins-Hughes; 92 Winfried Heinze (Designer: Grant White); 93 Winfried Heinze; 94 Kim Sayer; 95 Alun Callender; 96 Warren Smith; 97 Alun Callender; 98 Johnny Bouchier; 99 Grant Scott; 100 Paul Massey; 101 Richard Holt; 102 Warren Smith; 103 Helen Miller (Designer: Clare Nash); 104 Sandra Lane; 105 N Minh & J Wass; 106 Christine Bauer; 107 Jake Fitzjones (Designer: Shani Zion); 108 Winfried Heinze; 109 Victoria Gomez.

First published in 2010 by Conran Octopus Ltd, a part of Octopus Publishing Group, Endeavour House, 189 Shaftesbury Avenue, London WC2H 8JG www.octopusbooks.co.uk

A Hachette UK Company www.hachette.co.uk

Distributed in the United States and Canada by Octopus Books USA, c/o Hachette Book Group USA, 237 Park Avenue, New York, NY 10017 USA

Text copyright © Conran Octopus Ltd 2010 Design and layout copyright © Conran Octopus Ltd 2010

The right of Terence Conran to be identified as the Author of this work has been asserted by him in accordance with the Copyright, Designs and Patents Act 1988.

British Library Cataloguing-in-Publication Data. A catalogue record for this book is available from the British Library.

Consultant Editor: Elizabeth Wilhide

Publisher: Lorraine Dickey
Managing Editor: Sybella Marlow
Editor: Bridget Hopkinson

Art Director: Jonathan Christie
Picture Researcher: Liz Boyd
Design Assistant: Mayumi Hashimoto

Production Manager: Katherine Hockley

ISBN: 978 1 84091 551 8
Printed in China